Feb 19 2021

Reflections of Hope

A Devotional Journal for Those Loving Someone with Dementia

Reflections of Hope

A Devotional Journal for Those Loving Someone with Dementia

Heidi Dalton

Dedication

In memory of my precious mom,
Erna Edeltraud Kunkle,
the strongest and kindest woman I have ever known.
I love you, Mom. Until we meet again . . .

"Strength and dignity are her clothing,
and she laughs at the time to come.
She opens her mouth with wisdom,
and the teaching of kindness is
on her tongue."
—Proverbs 31:25–26

Contents

Acknowledgments

All praise to God, the One who sustains me, for planting this dream in my soul during my prayer time early one morning. You placed the words in my heart. I am returning them back to you for your glory.

Thank you to the love of my life, Jeff, my encourager, my strength, my support, my helpmate, and my soul mate. Thank you for believing in me and standing with me through it all. We're in this together, forever.

To our children, Zachary and Anna, thank you for supporting me, and for your sacrifice of time through the years for your grandmother who loved you dearly. I love you.

Introduction

This book is a devotional journal written to come alongside those who are caregivers, relatives, friends, or acquaintances of someone facing a dementia diagnosis. It is meant to be a safe place to process the full range of emotions we experience as we ride the waves of this disease.

I have chosen to keep this devotional general, using the term dementia because many diseases under the umbrella of dementia overlap and cause similar symptoms. Regardless of the root cause of our loved one's illness, we share a common bond in the feelings we experience as caregivers. Our paths will look similar and then become different many times during the journey of this disease as it ebbs and flows. No one's journey will be exactly the same as another, but we can glean much from the similarities.

I rode the roller coaster of dementia with my mom, who later succumbed to the disease. She needed to live her final eight months in a memory care facility, so I have written from the vantage point of having that experience with her. It had a profound impact on my life. Caring for my mother with dementia was one of the most painful journeys I have taken, yet it had moments of joy sprinkled in along the way. She continued to live and love until her final breath on Earth.

Because my mom was such a giver throughout her life, I honor her by sharing her journey in order to help someone else. In no way, shape, or form is this book written to replace medical or legal advice, or counseling if needed. It is the story of my walk with my mom, including what helped and what didn't. It is designed to be a friend to those who need a sympathetic ear and a place to vent, written by someone who's been there. Throughout the book I have interspersed excerpts from my personal journal entries and several of my own personal reflections. These writings are the "real me," often in the moment as I walked this path.

There are many facets to dealing with dementia. You cannot make this journey alone. You must reach out many times along the way. I was continually seeking information from other caregivers, attorneys, doctors, insurance experts, and I participated in a support group. Do your research. Explore different facilities at different times of the day. Observe how the nurses and aides interact with the residents in memory care. Write down your questions and be bold enough to ask them. An excellent place to start looking for help is your local Alzheimer's association. They can direct you to many helpful resources. Gather as much information as you possibly can.

By reflecting on your journey, alongside my reflections, I hope that this journal will in some small way help you know that you're not alone. But most of all, I pray that God will use it to lead you into his comfort, direction, and peace, and guide into the healing of your soul from the wounds that dementia inflicts.

What Is Happening?

The first realization that your loved one is changing is enough to take your breath away. The early symptoms of forgetting basic details, being afraid of the dark, not knowing how to handle money while buying groceries, not recognizing what to buy at the store even with a list in hand, exhibiting paranoia, and being unable to order from a menu were just a few of ours.

At first the changes are so subtle that we shrug them off until it gets to the place where we can no longer ignore them.

What changes did you first notice in your loved one's behavior? What were your thoughts at the time? When did you recognize that this was more than just "normal forgetfulness"?

Lord, changes are happening in my loved one. It is frightening and out of my control. Help me to trust in you as we continue on this ever-shifting journey.

> "When I am afraid, I put
> my trust in you."
> —Psalm 56:3

The Dreaded Diagnosis

The day comes in many forms. The doctor confronts your family member or you alone or all of you together with the dementia diagnosis. No matter what disease is causing the symptoms, the news is equally daunting. For me, Mom's doctor was out of town, so my husband and I were given the gut-wrenching task of telling my parents—a day that is burned painfully in my memory.

After receiving the phone call from the doctor's office, we drove to my parents' house, where my dad was sitting on the back deck in the sunshine. He was not well himself, being in his last stages of congestive heart failure. Mom was in the house. I spoke with Dad first, and then when Mom came out, we softly broke the news to her. My dad cried. Mom went over to comfort him, telling him it would be all right. She had no idea what was happening to her and didn't recognize or accept that she was even battling mind changes. I later found out that there is a medical term for that. It's called anosognosia, "lack of insight."

Where and how did you find out about your loved one's diagnosis? How did your loved one react? How did you feel at the time?

_____

_____

_____

_____

_____

_____

_____

_____

_____

_____

_____

_____

_____

_____

_____

_____

_____

_____

_____

_____

Lord, the diagnosis of dementia in any form can feel frightening. Please help us to accept our new reality so we can focus on how to find help with what we are facing.

> "When you pass through the waters,
> I will be with you; and through the
> rivers, they shall not overwhelm you;
> when you walk through fire you shall
> not be burned, and the flame shall not
> consume you. For I am the LORD your
> God, the Holy One of Israel, your Savior."
> —Isaiah 43:2–3

Where Are We Headed?

With the internet and instant availability of a plethora of information, it is easy to become overwhelmed with symptoms or stages that we aren't dealing with yet. We then become consumed and borrow trouble from tomorrow. It's essential to gain knowledge, but it's also important to live in the present.

Where is your loved one currently? Describe any moments where you've grown anxious about the future. How can you stay focused on today without wasting the present worrying about the future?

Lord, help me to take one day at a time because all we have is today anyway. Help me to trust that you will be there tomorrow with whatever it brings.

"It is the LORD who goes before
you. He will be with you; he will
not leave you or forsake you. Do not
fear or be dismayed."
—Deuteronomy 31:8

Forgotten, Not Forgotten

After dealing with this disease for some time, one of my greatest fears became, "What if this disease overshadows everything to the point that I forget the mom I had most all my life?" I didn't want all the precious memories I had of my mom replaced by her battle with dementia or the struggles that came along with it. I began purposefully remembering her before dementia entered the picture.

Take a few moments and bring to mind some of your favorite memories with your loved one. It helps to look at old photographs of happy times together: vacations, birthdays, holidays, and graduations, to name a few. List your favorite memories.

Reflections of Hope

_____

_____

_____

_____

_____

_____

_____

_____

_____

_____

_____

_____

_____

_____

_____

_____

_____

Lord, please help me to remember, and never forget, my loved one and his or her true being, the one before the disease. Let me realize that what I see today is only a manifestation of symptoms.

"My flesh and my heart may fail,
but God is the strength of my heart
and my portion forever."
—Psalm 73:26 NIV

Out of Our Control

My mom had mild and manageable symptoms until my dad's disease of congestive heart failure became end-stage. It was then that she forgot how to use the stove and other appliances. She was still taking tender care of my dad, bathing him and helping him dress, right up until his death.

The week after his death, we noticed her rapidly changing. We were unable to help her return to a calm state of being on her own.

We needed to make the decision to get help for her by admitting her to the hospital, which we did. It was one of the longest days of my life. At the end of the day, I was heartbroken, weary, and distraught. I wished there had been another way.

What difficult care decisions have you had to make to get your loved one medical help? How did you feel on those days?

Reflections of Hope

_____

_____

_____

_____

_____

_____

_____

_____

_____

_____

_____

_____

_____

_____

_____

_____

_____

_____

Heidi Dalton

Lord, I want to make the best choices for my loved one, but this is so painful and full of uncertainty. Please guide me to make good, sound decisions as we progress in this journey.

> "The LORD will guide you always;
> he will satisfy your needs in a
> sun-scorched land and will
> strengthen your frame. You will
> be like a well-watered garden, like
> a spring whose waters never fail."
> —Isaiah 58:11 NIV

Remembering for Them
— My Reflections

Mom is in the hospital. For several days now, I've been viewing life through the lens of those who have dementia in various forms. This disease is cruel, and yes, I said disease. These people are not odd or strange. They are suffering from an illness, for which there is no cure. They are living out their histories right before our eyes, all of it: the good, the bad, the ugly, the trauma they endured as children, their fears, and their need for safety.

I've watched these precious souls pass me in hallways day after day, and if I'm fortunate enough, they stop to give me a glimpse into their lives of many decades ago. Their eyes, the windows to their souls, are beautiful. Their hearts hold memories of a day and time to which I cannot always relate, but I can relate to their need for love and security, compassion and understanding, a soft voice, and a calm smile. Some of them are living out this disease alone.

I sometimes think that our society and churches have become so youth-oriented that we are abandoning these warriors in their most significant time of need. May it never be.

"Do not cast me away when
I am old; do not forsake me when
my strength is gone."
—Psalm 71:9 NIV

Changing Homes

Mom remained in the hospital for ten days, which felt like an eternity. She was reliving her childhood history, which produced post-traumatic stress disorder symptoms coinciding with her dementia symptoms. She believed the nurses were guards standing in the doorways. She would whisper as we walked past the nurses station because she was afraid they would hear her. She was fearful of eating the food that wasn't prepared by someone she knew. Under the supervision of the nurses, she would call me in between visiting hours and tell me not to come because they would "trap" me too. The doctor worked steadily on adjusting some medications for her.

After several meetings with the social worker, it was deemed that Mom would need twenty-four-hour supervision, and we would need to find a safe place for her. We had only a matter of days to find a facility.

This is a time when significant decisions have to be made that in reality should take months, but you are only given a few days.

It was a nightmare whirlwind. I set up appointments and began the daunting task of searching for the appropriate memory care facility. After a final phone conversation with my eldest brother, the last facility we observed was the one we chose. Ironically, it was the one Dad had asked me to drive past before his death. He wanted to see if both he and Mom could move there. That gave me an odd sense of comfort knowing he approved. After all the details were arranged and settled, we moved Mom's clothes and furniture into her new "apartment," as we called it. I was numb. And we still needed to tell my precious Mom.

Admitting her to the hospital and choosing her memory care facility were, by far, the most heartbreaking, pit-in-the-stomach decisions I had to make.

Have you needed to make a choice for your loved one that went against every fiber of your being, yet you knew it was the only safe and compassionate thing to do? Describe the process for you.

Lord, help me realize that I can't fix this. What I can do is obtain the best help for my loved one in this situation and keep him or her safe, no matter how painful it is.

"God is our refuge and strength,
a very present help in trouble."
—Psalm 46:1

I Was There
— My Reflections

It was a sunny, warm Thursday in early August. We ran errands and stopped by the monument company to view the gravestones. Mom chose one that she liked, a double heart. She loved the stone color called Bahama Blue. After hearing that she had chosen the most expensive granite of them all, my mom quickly said, "Oh no, that is too expensive." I encouraged her to wait on making a decision. We didn't order it that day, but we did receive the quote so we could take it home and think about it. We stopped to grab a burger for our supper. It was a pleasant day together, in spite of the circumstances and the odd, sad nature of our list to complete for the day. *I was there.*

When we arrived home early evening, I was exhausted, so I changed and decided just to lounge for the evening, maybe do some reading. But Mom was unusually restless, moving around the house, rustling in drawers, cupboards, and walking in and out of her bedroom. I attempted to get her to sit down with me by turning on some of her favorite TV game shows, but she was too out of sorts. At around ten o'clock, I told her I was going to bed, thinking that maybe she would settle down also. We both retired for the night, her to her bedroom and me to the bedroom that belonged to my brothers when we were growing up. *I was there.*

I fell asleep, only to awaken around 6:00 a.m. the next morning to my mom's loud voice coming from somewhere else in the house. I walked to the kitchen to find my husband standing there. He told me Mom had said people were coming in the house stealing from her all night long, and she was agitated and restless. She wanted to walk by herself to the cemetery to be with her husband. For the next several hours, my husband and I tried unsuccessfully to calm her, attempted to get her to eat some breakfast, offered her the usual cup of coffee that she drank daily, all in an effort to get her to take her blood pressure and diabetes medicines. We thought maybe her sugar level was off. But she adamantly refused any food or drink or medication. *And I was there.*

I spoke softly to her in her bedroom, attempting to get a feel for where she was in her mindset. She said she had been up all night watching the front door for "those people who were coming to steal" from her. She was packing all of her paperwork, her jewelry, some money, Dad's wallet, and various other items into plastic storage bags. I asked her where she was taking all of her packed things, and she said that she was taking them "home." An arrow went through my heart. I asked her where her home was, and she answered correctly. But when I asked her where she was, she then said, "I'm not at home, I don't live here, and stop asking me stupid questions." I left coffee and toast on her dresser, hoping she would eat or drink something and walked out of the room. My heart sank with the reality of what was happening. *And I was there.*

After 9:00 a.m., we called her doctor, who was not available at the moment. I explained the situation and awaited a return phone call, all the while trying to keep Mom comfortable and calm. When the doctor's assistant returned the call, they informed me that Mom would need to be regulated on some medication that would require a hospital stay in the Senior Care Unit and that we would need to go through the emergency room to get her admitted. This sounded like a plan, except for the fact that my mom, who was usually so sweet and compliant, was in no uncertain terms refusing to go anywhere with us. We tried having my eldest brother call her. She declined. We tried kindly "tricking" her to go with us. She refused. We finally landed on calling her pastor to come and help us, thinking that someone outside of a family member could persuade her. We had to push the issue because, at one point in the middle of the chaos, Mom had taken a handful of pills, which she told me were her daily medications. The problem was her medications for the day were still in a pill-box on the kitchen table, and I had no idea what she had just swallowed. Fear struck us to the core. *And I was there.*

Her pastor, bless his soul, came. Mom was receptive to him being there but highly suspicious. He talked with her calmly, eventually convincing her to ride to the hospital with us. We did tell her we would need to go to the emergency room first to get her the help she needed. As my mom retreated to her bedroom to gather what she felt she needed to take with her, especially her purse so no one would steal it, my heart and stomach began to grasp the enormity of what we were doing and what awaited us. I felt sick. Her pastor agreed to ride to the hospital with us, my husband and me in the front seat, and Mom and him in the backseat. He and Mom chitchatted about various things as we drove there, which seemed to take forever. I could barely speak, and I could scarcely breathe. *I was there.*

Upon entering the ER, I explained to the nurse at the desk why we had come. They asked us to have a seat in the waiting room until they were ready for us. A security officer who had been a friend of ours for years offered a cold bottle of water, which I accepted to help keep myself grounded to some semblance of reality. Shortly we were called back to be with Mom, and so began a long afternoon of restlessness. She repeatedly sorted through her purse to make sure nothing was taken, and she kept saying she wanted to leave. The doctor told us that by five o'clock they would have her in a room. Jeff and I watched this nightmarish scene as my precious mom looked at me and asked, "You're not sending me to a nursing home, are you? If that's why you have me here, and that's what this is all about, I'm not going." Another piece of my heart crumbled and broke to pieces. *And I was there.*

At last, it was close to seven when her room was ready. They had fed her supper, the doctor had apologized for the long wait, and we were heading down the long, echoing hallways to her place in the Senior Care Unit.

Upon arriving at her room, security made sure her money was counted in her purse in front of the nurse and us, then explained to her that it would all have to be locked up. She had been carrying a lot of money around with her, which none of us realized. Mom insisted that the security guard take a Christmas card that my dad had given her, which was also in her purse, and lock it up with her money. The officer seemed puzzled, and I merely said, "It's a treasure to her. Please take it with you." Another piece of my heart fell away. *And I was there.*

After what seemed like thousands of questions from the intake nurse, my husband and I walked out of the locked unit, leaving my mom and her confusion behind those closed doors. I will never forget the feeling I had as I left her there. Jeff and I had not eaten since early that morning. We were hungry, exhausted, emotionally drained, and distraught. I numbly told my husband, "Take me to my dad's grave." He drove me to the cemetery. My dad's grave was still fresh with flowers and piled high with dirt from his funeral only the week before. I fell to my knees and wailed. All I could manage to say was, "I'm so sorry, Dad, I'm so sorry. I wanted to take care of her." *And I was there.*

Throughout the next ten days of her hospital stay, Jeff and I spent many hours comforting and convincing Mom that it was safe to eat the food there. We tried to reassure her she was safe because her mind kept reverting in a post-traumatic stress disorder fashion to her war-torn childhood. We walked the halls and sat in the lounge area with her to make sure she didn't feel abandoned. We learned that she would need twenty-four-hour supervision, and my world completely shattered. *I was there.*

Over the next few days, I researched three different facilities. I also gathered as much information from my friends who are medical personnel in the area before deciding on which facility to place my mom. I spoke with my brother to get his thoughts. As many caregivers know who have been through this, multiple events happen rapidly that should be planned over months, but we are forced to evaluate and come up with solutions in a matter of days instead. At the same time, we were processing the emotions surrounding the fact that Mom couldn't come home again. *And I was there.*

I had the sickening job of telling my mom that she would be going somewhere else instead of her home, although we told her we would see how she did there. She wasn't happy, and neither was I. I didn't ask for that job and didn't want that job, but quite frankly this was only the beginning of doing many tasks that weren't comfortable and countless jobs I didn't want. *I was there.*

The director of the facility was more than accommodating. To make Mom's move more comfortable, she volunteered to pick her up at the hospital herself with another staff member. She knew that Mom was afraid of men and would be terrified of being transported with any males involved. So on a Monday morning, they went to the hospital, picked her up, stopped to get her ice cream on the way back, and settled her into her new home: the locked unit of a memory care facility. My mom was not able to leave with me to go to lunch or breakfast because I would have never been able to get her back there. It was the most horrific time of adjusting to the reality of this disease born out of hell. The pain and tears were stinging my soul and my eyes. *And I was there.*

The questions, some of which remain to this day, haunted my mind: Why couldn't Mom's mind stay stable so I could have enjoyed her in a normal way like other daughters enjoy their mothers after their dad has passed away? Why was I dealt the pain of not being able to bring her with me, but having to say good-bye to her as she asked me to go "home" every time I saw her? Why couldn't she have been pleasantly confused instead of having her nightmare of a childhood come back to haunt her? The questions were endless, and so was the anguish. *And I was there.*

"She Looks Fine to Me!"

For as long as I can remember, my mom always did her own hair. She only went to a beauty shop maybe once or twice. She had a talent for cutting, perming, and coloring it herself. She kept herself impeccably put together. She was so beautiful, both inside and out. She was able to keep up her self-care for a time in memory care, so it wasn't long after moving Mom to the facility that the questions from other people started. It would usually happen during a phone call or a happenstance meeting at a store while I was running errands. "Why did you move her? I went to visit her, and she looks fine to me!" Needless to say, after dealing with Dad's death so recently, then the heartbreak of Mom's mental changes, these judgmental attitudes from others were beyond agonizing. They came from people who never saw her in the hospital and had no clue what had been happening.

I tried to be kind and realize that people were speaking from lack of knowledge. But I also kept wondering, "Didn't people know me well enough to understand that I hated this too? Didn't they realize I needed to do what was best for her?"

There are times when we need to accept God's love and acceptance of us and disregard the opinions of others who have only a partial perception of what is happening. This is when we need to narrow down our circle of friends. Keep those close who will not drain you any further. Allow others to become a bit distant. You don't have to answer every phone call or every question. A simple "Please pray for us" will suffice. You'll need strength for the road stretching out before you.

What ridiculing or judgmental comments have you faced? Are you able to reject those in your mind and live in the truth of what you know is best?

_____

_____

_____

_____

_____

_____

_____

_____

_____

_____

_____

_____

_____

_____

_____

_____

_____

Heidi Dalton

56

Lord, help me to know in my heart that most others do not understand what we are living through or why we need to make these decisions. Help me to live in your truth guided by your love for us.

> "'The LORD is my portion,' says my
> soul, 'therefore I will hope in him.'"
> —Lamentations 3:24

Support for a Lonely Path

The journey with your loved one can be incredibly lonely. But it doesn't have to be if we realize that some relationships will come from unexpected places in unexpected ways.

I joined the support group at our facility. I found it very helpful, even though I couldn't attend every month. If you are open about dealing with your loved one's diagnosis, you will see that others who have dealt with similar diagnoses will step up and relate to you. I had some wonderful ladies who would send a card, write a text, or call me just because they had been there, too, and they understood. Look for people God is placing in your path whom you might not expect.

Who around you is also walking this journey or has walked it before? Are you able to reach out to them for support? Are you willing to do so?

Reflections of Hope

_____

_____

_____

_____

_____

_____

_____

_____

_____

_____

_____

_____

_____

_____

_____

_____

_____

_____

Lord, help me to recognize the safe people you place in my path. May they walk with me on this journey and ease my loneliness. Help them to reach out to me and me to reach out to them.

"Praise be to the God and Father
of our Lord Jesus Christ, the Father
of compassion and the God of all
comfort, who comforts us in all our
troubles, so that we can comfort those
in any trouble with the comfort we
ourselves have received from God."
—2 Corinthians 1:3–4 NIV

Sleepless Nights

Several weeks after Mom began living in memory care, she had her first of several falls, resulting in a gash to the back of her head. It required our first trip to the emergency room from the facility. They transported her by ambulance, and I met her there. I learned very quickly that ERs are not dementia friendly, for the most part. Once in a while, we were blessed with a nurse who knew what to say and what not to say, but some did not know or understand.

The doctor stitched her up; then the nurse called the ambulance for a transport back to the facility. The whole process confused and agitated Mom so much. I went home and caught a few hours of sleep before returning to sit by her side in the morning. It was exhausting, but I hated to leave her alone for too long after such an upsetting night.

There were many urgent phone calls like this in the middle of the night. It is incredibly unnerving to go to bed wondering if your loved one will be safe through the night. Panic would awaken me every time my phone rang. I always had clothes ready in case I needed to run out in a hurry, and I often slept with one eye open. Many long nights turned into long days. I learned to pause and take a few moments of rest wherever I could throughout my day because we just never knew.

Have you experienced emergent phone calls or situations with your loved one? What steps have you taken to be prepared?

_____

_____

_____

_____

_____

_____

_____

_____

_____

_____

_____

_____

_____

_____

_____

_____

_____

God, help me to be as ready as I possibly can for the critical times that arise. Please afford me rest in between and continued strength when needed.

> "In peace I will both lie down
> and sleep; for you alone, O LORD,
> make me dwell in safety."
> —Psalm 4:8

Shelter
— My Reflections

My mom, as she races around the memory care center, is continually looking for shelter and safety. Sadly, at this stage of her disease there is little ability left for her to feel those things. Her mind is fooling her into believing she is living in a different time and place, one in her past where she was unable to be safe.

I, too, am seeking shelter, as I face my dad's death, my mom in memory care, and now the sale of my childhood home. It isn't the first time I've needed emotional shelter. There have been many times in adulthood that I have felt the need to be sheltered from life's harsh realities. If we're honest, I believe we would all say the same thing. We long for shelter. We beg for it and cry out for it. We desperately need shelter.

May God be our shelter. May we also allow him to provide shelter through us to others around us who may need it.

"Whoever dwells in the shelter
of the Most High will rest in the
shadow of the Almighty."
—Psalm 91:1 NIV

I Want to Take Her Home with Me

One of the most painful experiences dealing with dementia is when your loved one wants to go home with you after you've been visiting. But you can't take them.

We would start preparing well in advance of our time to leave. We made sure Mom had something to drink, that she was settled in, and we tried to leave her either in the dining area surrounded by others or comfortably in her room sitting in her recliner with music playing. It didn't always work. As time went on, it rarely worked. Mom would walk so close beside me towards the door wanting to go "home," although where "home" was in her mind was continually changing. I can still picture her anguished face: lost, confused, angry, and sad. Sometimes an aide or nurse would attempt to distract her as I left. I wanted to grab her and run away from the unit, away from locked doors, and, most of all, away from this wretched disease. I couldn't. And it broke my heart many times over.

I would then swipe my key fob on the door frame. I always turned to look at Mom one last time, blew her a kiss if she was watching, and walked out the door of her memory care unit. Once on the other side of the clicking lock, my tears would break loose and flow freely.

How have you dealt with the pain of feeling like you're leaving your loved one behind? Have you let it release from your heart and out of your eyes?

_____

_____

_____

_____

_____

_____

_____

_____

_____

_____

_____

_____

_____

_____

_____

_____

_____

_____

Abba Father, please help me to be able to release the flood of pain and tears to you. It profoundly hurts that I can't bring my loved one home with me. You are the only One who can comfort this agony.

"The LORD is near to the
brokenhearted and saves the
crushed in spirit."
—Psalm 34:18

The Outpouring
— My Reflections

The world of living with a loved one who has one of the diseases characterized under the umbrella of dementia is, at times, nothing short of grueling. Oh, the countless times I've wanted to bring her home, the tears I've cried leaving her. The process of having an aide or nurse distract her after I tell her I'll check on her later so I can get out the locked door of the unit. The fear on her face at times, as she relives her past and no one can enter into that time and space with her where her mind lives at that moment to relieve her pain. The heartache of watching her roaming the hallways looking for a familiar place and time that no longer exists in the safety of her parents, or when she talks to her husband who is no longer living as though he were sitting there right beside us. The outpouring of love and emotion as she hugs me, placing her head on my chest, and says, "Your heart is beating," then stays there, calmly, in that moment. The inside tears as I get her dressed in her nightgown and tuck her safely in bed with a kiss good night on her forehead. How the roles have so drastically reversed. The not knowing how she will be when I walk into memory care and if I will find my mom as an adult, a child, confused, pleasant, agitated, paranoid, happy, crying, laughing, hiding, angry, calm, or fearful. The trial and error of medication changes to try to calm her, only to watch the vicious side effects take their toll on her body. The anger and sadness I feel that someone who served and loved others so freely her entire life is now trapped in this mind prison and suffers so greatly at times.

An Advocate for Life

Our loved ones living with dementia are still people. They lose abilities, but it does not diminish their value or worth. We are their advocates for life, not only for their needs but also for what makes them happy and comfortable in each stage.

You will need to be strong and speak for your loved one's best interests, regardless of whether people like you or not. There will be times when facility employees, hospital staff, friends, and family members don't appreciate your choices and feedback. That is to be expected. It is valuable to establish a good give-and-take relationship with whoever is in charge of your loved one's care. You will need a safe place to voice concerns when needed. I was fortunate to have this relationship with our memory care facility, and most concerns were taken care of promptly.

Do you have someone you can speak with freely as you advocate for your loved one? What kinds of encounters are you having, good and bad, with others who are taking care of your loved one? How are you resolving issues that arise?

_____

_____

_____

_____

_____

_____

_____

_____

_____

_____

_____

_____

_____

_____

_____

_____

_____

Lord, please provide me with wisdom and the right relationships so that I can honestly and effectively advocate for my loved one. Surround me with professionals who care and can offer helpful insight.

"On the day I called, you answered me;
my strength of soul you increased."
—Psalm 138:3

Breathe!

No matter how big or small the moment is when you choose to breathe, it's imperative to make it happen!

It might be driving to a local park and sitting in your car for ten minutes before or after a visit. It could be getting an ice cream cone or dining out for a break from cooking. My husband and I would stop at one of our favorite eateries and dine on the patio for some fresh air. Even a fast-food hamburger felt like a luxury some nights. Maybe it is sitting alone in your bedroom listening to music for five minutes to calm yourself or taking a long, hot bath. If your loved one is at home, it might mean having someone come over for fifteen minutes while you take a quick walk. Whatever it looks like, however long or short the time is, make it a priority to pause and breathe. It can feel like you're drowning and things might get blurry when surrounded by everything this disease offers up in a day. You need to come up for air, even for the briefest of moments.

Are you doing anything to help you catch your breath? If not, what is one small thing you can implement this week?

God, this is an exhausting journey. Please give me ideas and the means to refresh my soul from time to time so I can remain a healthy caregiver.

"Come to me, all you who are weary
and burdened, and I will give you rest."
—Matthew 11:28 NIV

Springtime on a Winter's Day
— My Reflections

We're in the middle of a typical March. In Ohio the weather can be quite unpredictable no matter what month we're in. It starts getting cold and snowing as early as October but usually closer to the end of November or beginning of December.

Everyone here gets excited for those first fluffy snowflakes to fall from the sky, as we are preparing for Thanksgiving and Christmas celebrations. There's just something about the first snowfall of the season. Then comes January when it turns bitterly cold, and we break out the snowblowers and shovels. We tolerate this cold, snowy season through January and February, but when March arrives, we are anxious for spring to come. The thrill of the first snow has worn off long ago, and we are getting tired of bundling up to go outside. The only problem is that in Ohio winter usually stretches on for a bit longer with an ebb-and-flow pattern of temperatures in the twenties and thirties, but occasionally a day here and there reaches fifty degrees, just enough to tease us. It stays gray for days on end here. When the sun peaks through, we almost have to remind ourselves of what that big bright orange-yellow ball in the sky is.

Last week was a week much like this weather-wise. The problem was that it was also a tough week for Mom. She had taken yet another turn, becoming very afraid; her paranoia was peaking, and her agitation had returned. She had reverted to reliving the atrocities she had endured as a child. The smiling, always positive Mom that I had known my entire life was hidden again behind a dark cloud in this horrid disease. I was tired. I was questioning, "Why would the Lord make one of His dearest servants relive trauma? How do we bring her relief? How do we adjust medication, lifestyle, words, and actions so we can comfort her?" The questions were endless. Sleep for me was scarce.

My husband and I had tickets to go to a praise concert about an hour away from where we live. I started questioning whether we should even go and if Mom would be okay. We decided to go anyway, knowing that the facility would call if they needed me and also knowing that I needed to worship. Worship feeds my soul. We went, we worshipped in a packed house full of other worshippers, and God met me there. He didn't take away Mom's symptoms or change the circumstance, but he comforted me in the depths of my heart, as I lifted my hands and let him meet my many needs. It's a pattern I find in Scripture over and over again, especially in the Psalms. David cried out to God repeatedly, questioned, agonized, and then he worshipped. I notice myself following the same pattern.

"O God, you are my God; earnestly I
seek you; my soul thirsts for you; my
flesh faints for you, as in a dry and
weary land where there is no water. So I
have looked upon you in the sanctuary,
beholding your power and glory.
Because your steadfast love is better
than life, my lips will praise you."
—Psalm 63:1–3

Mom, Are You in There?

When first arriving to visit Mom, we could usually tell a lot about how she was doing just from where we found her in the unit. Was she visiting with other residents at the tables? Was she lost in someone else's room? Was she walking the halls aimlessly? Was she sitting alone in her room, hesitant to open her door? Did she rush towards me when we came, appearing frightened or agitated? Did she whisper? Her facial expressions also gave us clues. Was she smiling? Did she have a blank stare?

There were so many times when I would watch her and wonder where she was mentally. I wondered how I could reach into her mind and find her for the day to understand what she needed. What was she thinking? Where was she living at the moment? How could we bring some joy to her today? *Mom, are you still in there?*

Is it difficult for you to find your loved one some days? What methods have you found that help you discern what is needed for the day?

_____

_____

_____

_____

_____

_____

_____

_____

_____

_____

_____

_____

_____

_____

_____

_____

_____

Father God, so many times it looks like my loved one is lost inside his or her own mind. Please help me to meet the need whatever it is for today. Show me how to serve my loved one best in order to bring peace and comfort.

> "The LORD gives strength to
> his people; the LORD blesses his
> people with peace."
> —Psalm 29:11 NIV

Go Ahead and Laugh!

Let's be real here. There are moments in this journey that are just plain funny, if not downright hilarious. There's nothing wrong with finding humor in the middle of all this confusion.

There was the time Mom thought her toilet was a wastebasket and we found her medical alert necklace thrown in there, among countless other items. I will never forget the look on my brother's face. Then there was the time I was helping her into her nightgown, and she lay down on her bed laughing hysterically at me, so I lay down beside her and laughed with her. Those moments, along with countless others, are now sweet memories that make me smile.

Don't hesitate to make laughter a part of your journey. It lightens the burden of many difficult days.

What has your loved one done or said that has made you laugh? Have you enjoyed the moment together?

_____

_____

_____

_____

_____

_____

_____

_____

_____

_____

_____

_____

_____

_____

_____

_____

_____

Lord, please let me embrace the humorous moments you allow as a relief from the stressful days. Help us continue to laugh together for as long as we are able.

> "May the God of hope fill you with all joy and peace as you trust in him, so that you may overflow with hope by the power of the Holy Spirit."
> —Romans 15:13 NIV

A Walk in the Sunshine

My mom was an avid exerciser, and what she thoroughly enjoyed her entire life was walking. I made sure, whether she was at home, in the hospital, or in the memory care facility, that we kept walking. We walked miles upon miles in the hall-ways. We went outside to the courtyard in the warm sunshine, and when snowflakes were falling, I bundled her up and out we went. Many days this changed her mood and calmed her considerably.

What is something your loved one has always enjoyed? Music? Exercise? Gardening? Crocheting? Sewing? How can you find ways to implement these into your loved one's rou-tine? For your loved one's safety, some of these might need to be done under your supervision while you're visiting.

Lord, please give me creative ideas and ways to allow my loved one to continue doing what he or she has always enjoyed.

> "And my God will supply every
> need of your s according to his
> riches in glory in Christ Jesus."
> —Philippians 4:19

Ice Cream Treats and Smiles
— My Reflections

My mom has had a difficult time in her facility the past several weeks. I'm learning to keep a "distraction bag" that I can grab at any moment to take with me—with manicure supplies and a book or two or some sort of activity.

I usually start with a big hug for her, although she no longer engages in embraces. More often, she stands still and just lets me hug her, which tugs at my heartstrings since my mom has always been the most demonstratively loving person you could ever meet. Then I sit with her for a while, listening to her fears of people stealing her laundry or possessions, or her fear of being kidnapped or trapped. After that, I ask her to walk with me, stating that I haven't done my laps for the day. Well, lately we have accomplished all of these steps and then sat at one of the tables in the common area to visit or get out a distraction book. One day recently the staff was offering an afternoon snack, which happened to be that yummy child-hood treat consisting of a white, creamy ice cream center with an orange ice pop surrounding it. Mom decided she wanted one, so my husband and I sat there with her while she enjoyed it. She commented that it tasted so good and she had never had one before. Many times, due to the nature of this disease, she thinks she has never seen, tasted, or heard of something before. Sometimes that is a blessing in disguise because it creates a new, unique experience for her. Even something as simple as an ice cream treat.

For some reason, as I watched her smiling and eating her snack, it tugged at my heart. Maybe it was because something so simple was giving her a smile for the day or perhaps it was the realization of all this disease has stolen from us, but something in that moment made my heart ache deeply for her. At the same time, I was thankful for the blessing of a simple ice cream treat that put a smile on my beautiful mom's face.

Mourning Loss Upon Loss

The dichotomy of having your loved one physically present yet witnessing them fade away mentally is heartrending. There are many losses in this journey that need to be mourned along the way.

One such time for me was my birthday. My parents never missed a birthday, whether we lived near or far. My family was fortunate to celebrate every birthday, theirs and ours, together. Mom always loved celebrating. So when my birthday came around while she was in memory care, it was a significant change for me. We went and sat with her for a long time because I wanted to be with the woman who gave birth to me. I remembered, even though she did not. We never said a word about it. I just soaked up her presence. It hurt. Not because I was upset with her, but because in my mind I asked, "What kind of cruel disease causes your mom to forget her child's birthday? This disease is relentless."

What losses have you and your loved one experienced thus far? Has your loved one forgotten birthdays or holidays? Has he or she perhaps forgotten your name? Are you taking time to mourn the losses as they come?

Abba Father, help me to realize that it is healthy and normal to mourn the losses in my loved one as I once knew him or her. May I bring my losses to you for comfort and peace.

> "You have kept count of my
> tossings, put my tears in your bottle.
> Are they not in your book?"
> —Psalm 56:8

A Diet of Tears
— My Reflections

> "My tears have been my food day and
> night, while people say to me all day
> long, 'Where is your God?'"
> —Psalm 42:3 NIV

If you have been through anything significantly heartbreaking (and most of us have), you know what it's like to have a diet of tears—when you awaken with the disbelief that this reality has become yours overnight, and you have tears for breakfast. Then as you walk through the day, you can barely catch your breath as you deal with the pushing and pulling of your troubled mind, and you have tears for lunch. As you struggle to make it to the end of your day with literally no energy left, tears are your main course for supper, and finally you fall into a heap as the sun goes down on a pillow of tears for the night. A diet of tears. There are those experiences in life that leave us with no words, only the crying out to our heavenly Father and a diet full of tears.

I have always believed that tears are a gift from our heavenly Father. I cringe when people apologize for crying. God so masterfully gave us that pressure release valve of allowing the tears to flow out of the overflowing agony in our hearts and souls. It is a blessing to be able to cry. Thank you, Lord, for realizing we would need relief from what weighs us down.

> "Weeping may endure for a night, but
> joy comes in the morning."
> —Psalms 30:5 AMPC

Slow and Steady

This disease can make you question every decision you make. It can fool you into thinking you and the doctors were wrong. At times, we would walk in and my mom would seem like she was back to her old self, perfectly well. The roller coaster of emotions and questions would race through my heart and mind. But then after sitting with her a while, the disease would rear its ugly head once again.

I learned to take it slow, watch, observe, gain the knowledge of where she was in her mindset for the day, then enter into her world and live with her there. I would listen to her fears, then try to redirect her out of them with distraction. Sometimes it worked; sometimes it didn't. It took a lot of effort, discernment, and painstaking patience.

It's vital to learn to live in your loved one's reality while you're with them. Agree as much as possible. In the long run, it makes no difference if your loved one is right or not. It does make a world of difference if they are happy, though. It can make the visits much smoother.

What can you do differently to live in your loved one's world? Do you find it challenging to engage in conversations that are not currently reality? How can you change your perspective to be able to do that?

Reflections of Hope

Lord, help me to be able to recognize that all of the ups and downs are part of the disease. Help me to learn new techniques for communicating and relating to my loved one, realizing that the end goal is always comfort.

"I bless the LORD who gives me counsel; in the night also my heart instructs me. I have set the LORD always before me; because he is at my right hand, I shall not be shaken."
—Psalm 16:7–8

Nostalgia and the Holidays

The holidays can be emotionally challenging for everyone when dementia is involved. But there is also the potential to create new and pleasant memories. They will just be different than before. It is a good time to modify your expectations and simplify your celebrations. By not planning more than what can be accomplished peacefully, you can greatly lessen the stress burden for you and everyone else involved.

With each change that came about in my mom's mental state, it required us to adjust more and more. Mom didn't know when it was Thanksgiving or Christmas, but we still did. I longed for the celebrations that were living in my memory. We chose to make new memories by enjoying the Thanksgiving meal with her at her facility and participating in the Christmas party they sponsored. I took a small, tabletop tree in to Mom's room with some safe decorations, as well as a few familiar ones from Christmases past at Mom and Dad's house. We decorated that little tree one evening together. She enjoyed it, and so did I. It wasn't the same, and it was sad to lose some traditions, but at least we were still together.

How can you make it easier and less stressful for both you and your loved one during the holiday season? What can you do with your loved one safely that evokes warm memories?

Heidi Dalton

128

Lord, this disease robs us of many holiday traditions. Although it is sad for me, please help me adjust to our current reality and make new memories of our present moments.

> "Cast your burden on the LORD,
> and he will sustain you."
> —Psalm 55:22

Apple Strudel
— My Reflections

My mom was from Germany, and she was an excellent baker. As I was growing up, she would bake Apfelstrudel (apple strudel), and oh, what a delicacy it was! The aroma of fresh, always hand-grated apples baking in a flaky, rich pastry crust was enough to make my mouth water. It was her original recipe. I have not been able to find that exact taste in any slice of apple strudel that I have tried anywhere, in any restaurant, and believe me, I have searched! She had a special touch with an heirloom recipe. She shared countless platters of it with family, relatives, and friends through the years, and it always had to be delivered on the exact day she made it because it was the freshest then. She never wanted it to sit for even one day.

A Christmas party was held at the memory care facility, and each family could bring in their traditional dessert if we so desired. I decided to attempt making the infamous apple strudel to surprise my mom. I held a couple pieces back to take to her early before the party started. I gave her a piece and said, "Here, Mom, taste this." A huge smile spread across her sweet face, and she said, "Mmm, apple strudel." I asked her if it was good enough, and she said, "It's perfect."

There is a verse in the Bible that says, "Taste and see that the LORD is good; blessed is the one who takes refuge in him" (Psalm 34:8 NIV). The words remind me of that beautiful day with my mom and the satisfied, happy look on her face when she tasted something so familiar to her that brought her joy.

Our Lord is that good to us also. He fills us with not only our needs but even our desires at times, and definitely his strength and protection. He invites us to taste and see that he is good.

Utter Chaos

As we faced later disease stages, we never knew what to expect when we entered Mom's room. There were many days when it looked like someone had ransacked the place. She didn't recognize her clothes and wanted us or the staff to give them away. They would be hung all over her room, lying on the bed, piled in chairs, or scattered throughout the hallway. She started using hand creams on her lips and in her hair. I always took a deep breath after we knocked on her door before entering.

We spent hours and days repeatedly cleaning up her room, removing items that had become unsafe, securing her personal care items up out of reach, and putting all of her clothes back in closets and drawers. There was so much mental chaos for her, which manifested in physical turmoil. It was strenuous for us trying to stay ahead of it all, so we could only imagine how taxing it was for her.

What chaotic behaviors have you encountered with your loved one? How do you deal with the turbulent moments of this disease?

God, there is so much confusion and turmoil associated with the progression of this disease. Please help me to keep a level head and emotions, even when I need to fix the messes repeatedly.

"You are my hiding place and
my shield; I hope in your word."
—Psalm 119:114

Caught in the Middle
— My Reflections

Now and then I feel caught in the middle. I long to go back. I have that tugging on my heart and emotions to be a younger me again, the person full of dreams and goals with life stretching out in front of me with endless possibilities. The new bride dreaming of a family and a home. The young mom with small children running around her feet. The forty-year-old mom with her high schoolers, ballet recitals, and basketball games to attend, running wildly to keep up before my house became an empty shell of memories of days gone by.

As I sit with Mom and watch these beautiful women stuck in their minds, I can't help but wonder about all their longings and heart tugs to live in a younger time and space, and how they revert daily to attempting to live that out.

More and more, I look forward to the day in eternity when we're all free from the human longings that keep us unsettled.

That day when we're genuinely complete in Christ and entirely free from the bondage of our mortal bodies, desires, and feelings. That transforming time when we're all made whole and brand-new again. The day when we will spend forever basking in the glorification of God.

Dignity, Respect, and Pampering

As my mom's abilities were slipping away, there were several areas that I was adamant about retaining on her behalf: her dignity and respect, and pampering her to the fullest.

When we would go for a visit, which became multiple times a day, I would always go in first, before anyone else, to make sure she was fully clothed. If she was in the dining area, I would take a quick inventory of her as I walked in to see if she had everything she needed. There were times when her eyeglasses or an undergarment would be missing or she had her shoes on without socks. I made sure to take her to her room and finish whatever needed to be done so she would feel complete. She was always meticulous about that, and I wasn't about to let that change just because she was unable to remember everything she needed. She would always say, "That feels better," so somewhere in her mind, I knew she could tell, even if she couldn't verbalize it. I made sure we still respected her and gave her as many choices as possible. Mom liked diet cola and water. Instead of asking her what she wanted, we found it best to ask, "Would you like diet cola or water?" It still gave her control but aided in her decision.

My other goal was always to pamper her. I made up a bag of hair and nail supplies. She loved it. She often fell asleep in her rocker while I was curling and brushing her hair. My dear husband would clean her glasses. I would then put her favorite cream on her face since she was unable to use that properly by herself anymore. She remembered the fragrance, and it smelled good to her. I trimmed her toenails and rubbed in her foot cream. I would unwrap a piece of her dark chocolate and give it to her to eat. She didn't recognize what they were anymore in the wrapper, but she loved the taste. Appealing to her pleasurable senses was always a positive experience when nothing else worked anymore. She might have forgotten what we did, but she felt good, and that remained.

How are you making sure that your loved one is still given dignity and respect? Are you able to come up with ideas to pamper him or her and appeal to what brings about good feelings?

Reflections of Hope

Heidi Dalton

Heavenly Father, my loved one is still able to taste, smell, hear, touch, and see. Please help me to value and maintain my loved one's dignity and respect, plus bring pleasure to our time together with the good gifts you give.

"Every good and perfect gift is from above, coming down from the Father of lights with whom there is no variation or shadow due to change."
—James 1:17

Gargantuan Guilt

There certainly seems to be a surplus of guilt felt by caregivers. I, too, felt the weight of guilt, especially at the beginning of the decision-making process. It intensified when we needed to place our family home up for sale because our funds for Mom's care were quickly running out. The doctor reiterated to me that Mom could never go back home.

Our home—the house my dad had built, the home where we grew up and where our children also played in the backyard. What felt like it would destroy me was when Mom saw a picture of her house advertised in the local newspaper, and she recognized it. She was infuriated with me, and I couldn't blame her. Most days, she didn't remember where she lived or if she was back at her childhood home in Germany. Sadly, this had to be the one time she knew her house when she saw it. I was overwhelmed with guilt for having to take this step in her care, although I had no alternative.

Another guilt burden was that even though I tried to stay on top of my behavior around Mom, there were days when I didn't say the right thing or react the right way and she would become agitated or distressed. I would realize it right after the words came out of my mouth, and I would immediately feel terrible. None of us is perfect in the way we deal with this wearing disease day in and day out. You have to be able to give yourself grace, learn from your mistakes, and try again.

Have you felt the weight of guilt in this process, even though you were doing what was necessary or simply doing your best in the moment? Which decisions or situations weigh on you the most? How can you reconcile those in your heart and mind?

Dear Lord, as a caregiver, I am often forced to do hard things so my loved one is in the best of care. Help me to remember that some decisions are necessary. Please comfort my heart in the choices that are so agonizing. May I also give myself a measure of grace and mercy on the days I'm not at my best.

> "Let us then with confidence draw
> near to the throne of grace, that we
> may receive mercy and find grace
> to help in time of need."
> —Hebrews 4:16

Selling the Family Home — My Reflections

I've been sitting here in the house that our family, through the generations, has called home for the last fifty-plus years. I can see my mom in the kitchen hand-grating apples and rolling out her apple strudel, humming as she bakes. She stops and teaches me how to roll it out just so, thinly, and then roll it back up, filled, to bake it perfectly before slicing. Mom gives me a taste of the sweet, spiced apples, just enough to whet the appetite of a small child waiting for the delicacy to come out of the oven. The aroma of cinnamon, nutmeg, and apples fills the air. She is making multiple batches so that she will be able to send a platter to the neighbors or an elderly person down the street or to someone sick and shut in. When it is done baking, we will let it sit until cool, after which we will sprinkle a dusting of confectioners' sugar on top. I can almost taste it now.

I walk the backyard where the swimming pool used to be. Many hours of laughter were shared in that pool with my siblings, my parents, and neighbor kids who needed to be cooled off. I can see my dad in the yard playing softball or badminton for hours with my children when they were young. We spent much time working together in that yard, each one of us—mowing the grass and trimming branches and picking apples off the golden delicious apple tree. I just harvested the last zucchini and okra from Dad's garden, as it's about to fade into autumn, then winter.

I walk past and run my hand across the dining room table where many homemade meals were served. We always gathered as a family at the table, and my mom was a fantastic cook. Prayer was never forgotten; we were ever thankful for what we had before us. We prayed, talked, argued, and laughed at that table. We were a family, and that's what families do.

I take a seat in my dad's recliner in the living room. I'm flooded with memories of endless gatherings and holidays; my children are sitting on the floor with their grandparents playing games, with Grandma (my mom) allowing them to touch the ornaments on the Christmas tree as she plugged in the lights. She always thought nothing was more precious than people, so go ahead and touch, feel, learn . . . things are replaceable. "Money is replaceable," Dad would even say. There was always music playing in this room while my mom cleaned or baked.

I remember my dad's very bright mind, his hearty laughter that persisted until his last day on Earth, and my mom's unfailing love and devotion to her God and her family. I remember the joy on my parents' faces when the newest precious great-granddaughter would arrive for a visit. These walls hold lifetimes of memories, but more importantly, my heart holds them: a treasure box of priceless moments with those I have loved.

Parting with Memory Containers

Memory containers . . . that title came to me as I signed the final papers to close the sale of my parents' home. Some would say it was just a house, and the memories are in your heart. That's true, but that home was also a memory container for me. With tears, I ran my hands along every wall and space that I could for one last touch of the place where I grew up. That home was in our family for fifty-three years.

Our children played baseball and helped Grandma and Grandpa pick up sticks in that backyard. We all picked yellow delicious apples from their apple tree clear on the back of the property. The deer would walk to the apple tree to have their snack, and the birds would flock to one of my dad's favorite things, his bird feeder. But on this day my heart broke as I took a final walk through the backyard and the house.

It was a winter day in Ohio, not one of our usual frigid days, but a little sun shining through and a stiff breeze blowing. Nothing was blooming or growing, and it merely looked dead and barren to me. And in all honesty, I felt a bit numb and barren too.

My mom was sitting in a memory care facility, not even realizing that her house had just been sold. How does a daughter do that and feel good about it, even though the circumstances made it necessary? Those of you who have had to cross this bridge will understand the angst this creates in heart and mind — two different memory containers. My mom's memory container, her mind, is fading. The house memory container is gone out of our possession now. So now my heart becomes the memory container keeping it all safe and sound.

Letting go of material items can be difficult when they remind you of happy times and special people in your life. Have you found it necessary to sell a home or possessions that belonged to your loved one and held sentimental value for you? What steps can you take to release those physical memory containers, yet continue to hold those memories and feelings close in your heart?

Caring Father, I am finding it painful to let go of material goods that seem to take my loved one with them. Please help me to release what needs to go and realize that what is truly precious is held in my heart for eternity, and no one can take that away.

"But lay up for yourselves
treasures in heaven, where neither
moth nor rust destroys and where
thieves do not break in and steal.
For where your treasure is, there
your heart will be also."
—Matthew 6:20–21

Today Is Enough

Most of the time, Mom was frightened and living in the past, but there was a window of time where she became pleasantly confused—almost giddy. It was a three-week period right before she took her final downturn. She was living in a portion of her past when her life was full and happy.

She would chat with my dad as if he were sitting next to her, talk to her parents as if they were still alive, ask me how my babies (who are now adults) were doing, and so on. She would laugh easily and often. Even though she wasn't living in the present, I treasured those days. She was carefree for a time.

Jeff and I chose to accept that each day was enough. We laughed with her and just soaked up the reprieve from fear and anxiety that she was enjoying. I also found it helpful to focus on something from that day for which I could be thankful.

In the middle of all the turmoil, are you able to have moments or days where you understand that today is enough? List three things about today for which you can give thanks.

Abba Father, I am so grateful for the days that offer a smile and a bit of relief. Help me to make the most of those happy moments with my loved one, living in the moment and allowing tomorrow to take care of itself.

> "Therefore do not worry about tomorrow, for tomorrow will worry about itself. Each day has enough trouble of its own."
> —Matthew 6:34 NIV

Still A Giver

My precious mom was a giver her entire life. She was always baking for someone or taking a meal to a family in need. She made countless casseroles for funeral dinners at their church. Her giving nature stayed with her, even when her memory was fading. She wanted to help take care of other residents in the facility, whether helping them eat or move around safely.

She also always liked little caramel candies, so either my brother or my husband and I would keep her supply stocked. We noticed that they were disappearing rapidly, and we wondered how on Earth she was eating all that candy in a day! We later found out she would stuff the pockets of the staff with them. She also loved having something to give our children when they visited. It made her feel like she still had a purpose.

What endearing qualities of your loved one still shine through in spite of the disease? How can you continue to encourage these?

Heidi Dalton

Lord, I am thankful that my loved one still holds on to some precious qualities unique to him or her. Watching those shine through brightens my days with familiarity.

> "Rejoice always, pray without ceasing,
> give thanks in all circumstances;
> for this is the will of God in
> Christ Jesus for you."
> —1 Thessalonians 5:16–18

What's Yours Is Mine?

Anyone familiar with dementia knows that things will come up missing from time to time or new items will suddenly appear!

Every so often, I would notice another lady wearing one of Mom's sweaters or Mom would have some "new" piece of clothing in her closet. I realize this can be a bigger problem, but we never kept anything of great value in my mom's room, other than her wedding rings and a few pieces of jewelry she had always worn and would not take off. I was not about to take those from her, and if they became lost, then they would just be lost. Mom had complained repeatedly about other residents stealing the silverware from the dining room. We later found several sets of cutlery tucked in between her clothes in her dresser, which made us laugh.

Also, for as long as I can remember, my mom loved her Bible. She faithfully read it daily. She was always so proud when my dad would buy her a new one. It was such an endearing trait about her.

Every once in a while, we would notice a different Bible in her room at memory care. We'd smile to ourselves. We affectionately said that Mom was "collecting" Bibles. By the time we were clearing out her drawers, we had discovered several hidden, which we made sure were returned to their proper owners. It is one of my fondest memories recalling her "Bible collector" abilities.

Has your loved one "collected" anything that brings a smile to your face? If so, what are those items and why are they meaningful to your loved one?

Lord, many behaviors go along with dementia that I can't control. Help me to take them lightly and smile upon the things that won't matter in the long run.

> "The steadfast love of the LORD never ceases; his mercies never come to an end; they are new every morning; great is your faithfulness."
> —Lamentations 3:22–23

The Time Has Come

As the days passed and seasons changed, my mom's looks and behaviors also changed. She didn't look or act like my mom. She seemed to age years in a matter of days. She began leaning to one side and then the other. She was falling more. She was extremely restless and agitated, and it got to the point where she was unable to sit still at all. The doctor tried medication changes. She would hide in her closet, fearful of coming out. I was there morning, noon, and evening, watching this disease—this horrific disease—ravage my mom's mind and now her body.

She rarely smiled. I could feel her slipping away. She forgot how to write and how to eat, and she was reverting into speaking her native language, German. I could understand some but not all of what she tried to communicate, definitely not enough. Then she became silent. No more words. No more hearing my mom's voice. It was all happening faster than any of us could grasp. She was fading from our presence.

Jeff and I had usually been able to calm her, but we were now losing our ability to do that too. She was leaving our world entirely. There was nothing more we could do.

She developed a fever on a Saturday with no other symptoms of illness. Her face was burning hot and red. I sat with her as she lay in bed, trying to keep her cool and attempting to figure out how to help her. She lost her ability to swallow. She was not communicating at all.

Finally, that evening, I decided to have her sent to the emergency room. I hated to take that step to move her once again, but we needed to know what was happening and how we should proceed.

On Monday morning during the brief hospital stay, the palliative care team, a kind nurse, and the chaplain entered her room. And I knew. Things were about to change drastically again.

Have you witnessed your loved one coming to end stages in this disease? If so, have you felt the dichotomy of wanting them finally free from dementia yet not wanting to let go? How is this influencing the decisions you need to make?

Reflections of Hope

Heidi Dalton

Abba Father, I know my loved one is in your care ultimately, but it is grueling to watch this disease overtake his or her mind and body. Please bring comfort and peace as my loved one slips from me into your loving arms and enters into your eternal presence without confusion or pain or tears. Fully healed and whole.

> "He will wipe away every tear from
> their eyes, and death shall be no more,
> neither shall there be mourning, nor
> crying, nor pain anymore, for the
> former things have passed away."
> —Revelation 21:4

Holding Vigil
— My Reflections

It has been necessary for me to hold vigil for someone who was dying twice now: once for my dad eight months ago, as he was passing away from congestive heart failure, and most recently for my mom who passed away five days ago.

She was hospitalized for flu symptoms about six weeks ago and never regained her stability mentally or physically after that, which is not uncommon for someone with dementia, but it is still unsettling to those of us caring for them.

Over the past three weeks, she began spiraling downhill in all ways, culminating in yet another hospitalization. My husband and I had gone to the hospital early on a Monday morning to sit with her when the palliative care team came in to talk with us. I wasn't surprised because I had told Jeff the week before that she looked like she was dying. You can tell, and after watching my dad go through this, I knew the signs.

We went into another room to discuss the plan for taking her back to her memory care facility under the care of hospice. I left that meeting with a sense of relief that she would be compassionately taken care of in her final days by them and us, just like my dad was, but also with reality hitting like a ton of bricks telling me I would have minimal time left with my precious mom, also just like with my dad.

The afternoon was a blurred rush of getting her room cleaned and set up, and preparing for her to return. I wanted it all done because once she returned, I would not leave her alone. It was time to hold vigil for the one who had done that for me countless times as her daughter. The previous weeks I had also held vigil for her during her times of intense fear. It's what love does, at least the love that I know.

My beautiful mom was returned to our care. I sat and took care of the woman who had taken care of many others through all the years of her life. As I listened to her breathing in the darkness of the night, I realized how blessed I have been to have had this woman as my mom. If I were to describe her in words, she has been a loving servant of God and a giver to everyone surrounding her. You couldn't be around her for even a few moments and not know she loved you. The words "I love you" flowed freely from her lips.

My husband stayed by my side. Our children came. My brother and his family arrived. We all took turns holding vigil for her, holding her hands, wiping her brow with cool cloths to calm her fevered body, positioning pillows under her for comfort and to prevent bed sores, keeping her lips moist, playing her favorite hymns of harp music softly in the background, reading Scripture, and whispering words of life, thanks, love, and comfort into her ears.

She was never left alone until she departed our presence and entered God's eternity that early Saturday morning at 2:00 a.m.

The entire process brought to mind how our heavenly Father holds vigil for us throughout our whole lives until we return to him: never sleeping, never tiring, always on guard, still protecting, and ever loving—always holding vigil for his children.

> "I lift up my eyes to the hills. From where does my help come? My help comes from the LORD, who made heaven and earth. He will not let your foot be moved; he who keeps you will not slumber."
> —Psalm 121:1–3

Unexpected Teacher

This entire journey has taught me much that I never anticipated learning.

I learned how to communicate with someone whose brain is no longer functioning like mine is. I learned how to be humble in placing my need to be right, last, and Mom's need to be understood and happy, first. I learned how to live in the moment, not in the past, nor the future, but the present moment. I learned how to return to enjoying the simple things in life. I learned, once again, the value of honoring and preserving our relationships with our loved ones today, because tomorrow might change everything. I learned to be flexible and not need to have all things planned out at all times. I learned how to keep myself healthy amid extreme stress through small acts of self-care. I learned to mourn losses as they come. I learned how to smile and laugh, even in hard circumstances.

This disease taught me a depth of love that I had never known before, a self-sacrificing love. Love that would go many extra miles even when I was tired. I learned to have a much higher dependence on God and his care for my loved ones. When all was out of my control, God was the only one who could take care of my mom.

I believe that, if we are open to it, there is always something of value to be taken from every hardship in life. As you near the end of this journal, ponder what your teachable moments from this disease have been thus far and write them out. Think about ways you can then use these lessons to help someone else down the road.

Heavenly Father, even though the journey has been excruciating, I know that you have a plan in all things. May I clearly see what you have taught me, and may it be used for your glory and someone else's good.

> "Carry each other's burdens,
> and in this way you will fulfill
> the law of Christ."
> —Galatians 6:2 NIV

Your Hand in Mine
— My Reflections

I have a picture of my hand covering my mom's hand. My husband took it for me the week before Mom went home to Jesus, while I was sitting with her trying to comfort her, yet she was also comforting me.

Every day now, at some point, I sit and gaze at that picture, and I remember. And I remember. And I remember. There's nothing like a touch to heal and reassure. I remember my mom's warmth and the feel of her hand in mine. It takes me back to a sweet spot in life where my parents still stood tall as "umbrellas" over my life, sheltering me from as much harm as was within their power. It soothes my soul to be able to "feel" her again, not just intellectually remember her. It makes me smile to know that she's at peace with her Lord.

There are times in life where we have to take God at his Word and ignore our feelings, but there are other times God allows us to feel his presence for our comfort:

When I'm out walking and I see majestic deer standing out in a field.

When a butterfly lands beside me, reminding me of my mom's freedom from her illness and the constraints of this life.

When the warm sun shines on my face after a long winter, reminding me of God's embrace on the hard days.

When I hear the simplistic beauty of a bird singing.

When I'm admiring flowers that have pushed through the ground, finally blooming after the earth has been frozen for months.

When I'm sitting in front of an ocean, reminding me of both God's power and his restraint, which he sovereignly uses in my life.

When autumn leaves have changed into a dazzling array of colors, showing me that change can be a beautiful thing.

When I see soft snowflakes gently falling through the dark sky and covering the earth with purity.

When the silence of a winter's night is reminding me to rest.

All of these are touches of God's presence for my comfort and yours also. Yes, I do believe there are times when God allows us to feel him and not just observe him. Oh, the goodness of God.

A Moment to Look Back

At the time that I am completing this journal, it has been a little over a year since Mom went home to Jesus. Writing it out for you has played a large part in my healing. There have been many emotions to work through. I repeatedly went back and replayed every decision we made, how it was made, and the timing of making it. The healing journey has been a process. I have mourned the loss of physically being in my mom's presence, yet I have also celebrated the fact that she is not trapped in fear anymore. Her mind and body are no longer deteriorating before our eyes. She is at home with her Lord and my dad. I continually pray that a cure will be found because a dementia-related illness leaves so much devastation in its wake.

If I could go back and do it over, I would still spend all of the same precious moments with her. Although it was exhausting and draining, I don't regret in the least being with her during those days. I missed many church services, events, and vacations. But I am thankful I made time to be with my beloved mom when she needed me most. I now look at the opportunity to be by her side as one of my most precious gifts from God. It was also the last gift of love that I could give to her before she left this world. And oh, how much she gave to me through this entire learning and loving process.

I hope that walking this reflection pathway with me has been a blessing to you and that you will find some healing in remembering your own journey. God is a God of restoration and hope. May you find his peace and strength along the way as your heart mends until you meet your loved one again.

"But they who wait for the LORD
shall renew their strength; they shall
mount up with wings like eagles;
they shall run and not be weary;
they shall walk and not faint."
—Isaiah 40:31

Reflections

_____

_____

_____

_____

_____

_____

_____

_____

_____

_____
_____
_____
_____
_____
_____
_____
_____
_____
_____
_____
_____
_____
_____
_____
_____
_____
_____